D0722574

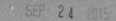

a gift for

_____

Blessed

Published by Sellers Publishing, Inc.

161 John Roberts Road, South Portland, ME 04106

Visit us at www.sellerspublishing.com • E-mail: rsp@rsvp.com

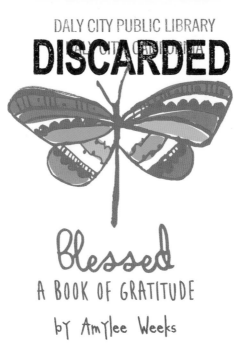

Blessed

A BOOK OF GRATITUDE

by Amylee Weeks

SELLERS
PUBLISHING

S

some everyday blessings . . .

- LAUGHTER —
IT IS CONTAGIOUS AND CURES HEAVY HEARTS

- PEOPLE WHO KNOW ME WELL AND LOVE ME ANYWAY

- SECOND, THIRD, FOURTH . . . CHANCES

- TECHNOLOGY —
IT ERASES THE MILES BETWEEN LOVED ONES

- A GOOD NIGHT'S SLEEP

be glad for
this moment,
for this moment
is your life.

be grateful for God,
who loves us
and has a plan
for our lives.

trust. believe. dream.

just when the caterpillar
thought the world was over,
it became a butterfly.

be thankful
that miracles
do happen
every day

be grateful that God
put so many people
in our lives
who care about us.

more everyday blessings ...

- THE ABILITY TO CREATE

- A GOOD LAUGH

- THE FACT THAT YOU CAN
TEACH AN OLD DOG NEW TRICKS

- THINGS THAT CHANGE

- THINGS THAT STAY THE SAME

- PERSPECTIVE

the more you thank life ...
the more life gives you
to be thankful for.

those who hope in the Lord
shall renew their strength.
they will soar.

be forever grateful
for hope.
it gives us
wings.

be thankful for
the ability to help
others in need ...
remember that
we are all in need.

when the world says give up,
hope whispers:
"try one more time."

be grateful
for second
chances

morning by morning,
new mercies i see.

peaceful blessings ...

- QUIET MORNING MOMENTS ALONE

- LOOKING THROUGH OLD PHOTOS

- THE SMELL AFTER A GOOD RAIN

- FINDING AN OLD JOURNAL

- A RAINY DAY, A GOOD BOOK,
  A COMFY COUCH, AND COFFEE

in the shadow of Your wings,
i will sing for joy.

PSALM 63:7

be grateful for
the chance
to follow your
dreams . . .
strive to conquer
your fears
of the unknown
with each step.

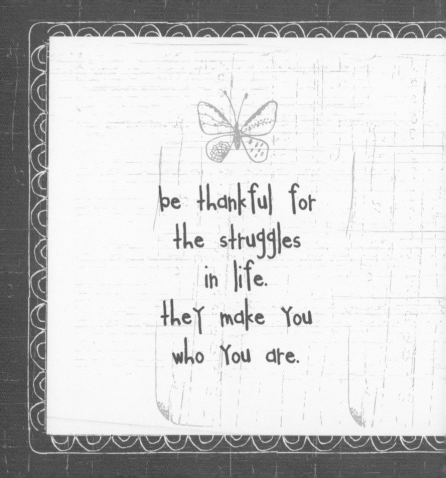

be thankful for
the struggles
in life.
they make You
who You are.

don't lose hope.

joyful blessings . . .

- BATHTUBS, SHOWERS, AND HOT WATER

- FIRST SIP OF COFFEE IN THE MORNING

- BIRDS CHIRPING

- A GOOD SONG ON REPEAT

- COMING HOME AFTER A LONG, HARD DAY

- COZY SOCKS

let go of yesterday,
appreciate the beauty
in today,
let grace seep in,
and soar.

love who you are.

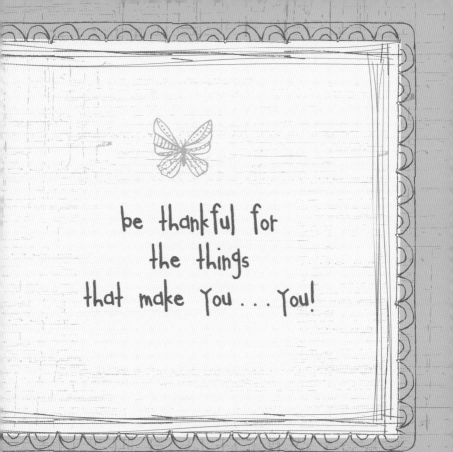

be thankful for
the things
that make You...You!

be grateful for
mistakes,
and the lessons
in forgiveness
and grace
they teach you.

let grace seep in.

be thankful for
the changing seasons —
they are the confirmation
that things
are meant to change . . .
and that's okay

embrace change.

seasonal blessings...

- HOMEMADE ROASTED PUMPKIN SEEDS

- THE CRACKLING OF A WARM FIRE ON A COLD NIGHT

- DECORATING A CHRISTMAS TREE

- TWINKLY LIGHTS

- THE FIRST SNOW OF THE SEASON

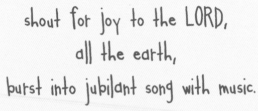

shout for joy to the LORD,
all the earth,
burst into jubilant song with music.

PSALM 98:4

stop the hustle
and bustle
of life.
for one minute,
step outside
and look around.
isn't it all
amazing?!

be grateful
for music —
the way it touches
the soul
and glorifies God.

live. love. sing.

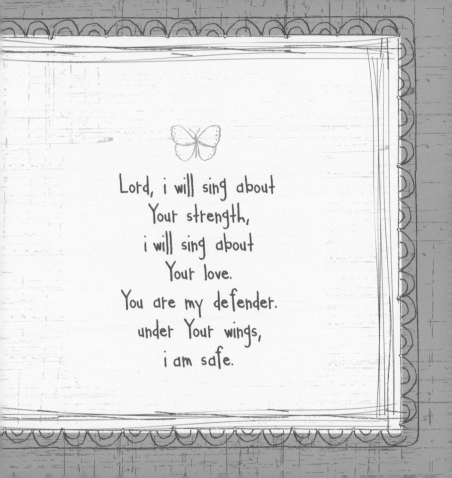

Lord, i will sing about
Your strength,
i will sing about
Your love.
You are my defender.
under Your wings,
i am safe.

music is the map to

so many memories.

be grateful
that one song
can bring back
so many
memories.

simple blessings...

- SOAKING IN A HOT BATH AFTER A STRESSFUL DAY

- THE SMELL OF FRESHLY BAKED COOKIES

- SLEEPING IN LATE

- LAZY DAYS

- GETTING LOST IN A GOOD BOOK

when life gives you
a hundred reasons to cry,
show life that
you have a thousand
reasons to smile.

be grateful that
joy can always
be found—even in
the most frazzled,
day-to-day
craziness of life.

the joy of the Lord is my strength.

A person with a
loving heart is blessed
with the power
to create happiness.

love anchors the soul.

be still and know.

be grateful that
one simple prayer
can quiet
life's chaos.

be blessed by
the silence
of the early
morning. it gives
the heart
the serenity it needs
to tackle
the day's tasks.

In the morning You will hear my voice, O Lord.
In the morning i will lay my requests before You,
and will watch expectantly. PSALM 5:3

natural blessings ...

- WISHING ON A DANDELION

- SHARING A SMILE
  WITH A STRANGER

- ICED TEA ON A HOT DAY

- AFTERNOON NAPS

- THE SNOOZE BUTTON

little things can make a big difference.

be grateful for
the teachers
who opened
our eyes
to so many
new worlds.

divine blessings ...

- CHERRY BLOSSOMS
  IN THE SPRING

- BIRDS CHIRPING

- FLOWERS BLOOMING

- THE SMELL OF
  FRESH-CUT GRASS

- A PINK SKY AT NIGHT

no matter how long
the winter,
spring always
arrives.

a garden of love
grows in a grandparent's
heart.

so grateful for
grace-filled,
loving hearts.

there is always, always,
ALWAYS
something to be thankful for.

gratitude is
concentrating more
on what you have,
rather than
what you don't.